The Girl's Body Book

By Kelli Dunham, R.N.

Illustrated by Laura Tallardy

APPLESAUCE PRESS

Applesauce Press is an imprint of
Cider Mill Press Book Publishers

This book may be ordered by mail from the publisher. Please include $4.95 for postage and handling. Please support your local bookseller first!

Books published by Cider Mill Press Book Publishers are available at special discounts for bulk purchases in the United States by corporations, institutions, and other organizations. For more information, please contact the publisher.

Cider Mill Press Book Publishers
"Where good books are ready for press"
12 Port Farm Road
Kennebunkport, Maine 04046

Visit us on the Web!
www.cidermillpress.com

Design: Alicia Freile, Tango Media
Typeset by Candice Fitzgibbons, Tango Media
Typography: Century Schoolbook, DIN, EdPS Gothic, Frutiger, Gill Sans, Grenouille, Johnny Script, Monotype Sorts

Printed in China

1 2 3 4 5 6 7 8 9 0
First Edition

TABLE OF CONTENTS

INTRODUCTION

Big Changes Ahead

What kind of changes? Well, lots of things.

The first thing you'll notice is that your body is changing. There are bumps where things used to be flat, and hair where things used to be smooth.

Then you might notice that your feelings are changing. Maybe you don't like the same things you used to, or maybe you feel happy or sad or tired or grumpy at strange times for no reason.

Finally you'll start to see your relationships changing. Boys start to act funny around you and your friends seem to be going through changes of their own.

Why all these changes? Well, you're growing up and entering a new phase of your life. Those of us who have been through it before know it can feel a bit like you're caught up

in a whirlwind sometimes. Just when it seems like you're getting really good at being a kid, you start to notice little changes in your body. Then you start to notice changes in the way you feel about yourself, your family, and your friends. In the meantime, maybe the grown-ups around you start talking about how you're "on your way to becoming a woman," even though no one even asked if you were done being a girl yet! Congratulations and welcome to the wonderful world of what's usually called "puberty." You might call it a pain in the neck. Keep in mind that while it can be a difficult time, it can also be very exciting.

We hope that this book helps guide you through some of the more challenging times ahead. And whether it was a gift or something you found at the bookstore yourself, it's yours now (well, unless you checked it out from the library) and that means you get to read it however you want. You might have questions that this book can answer, especially about what is happening now with your body and what is going to happen next. You can read just the parts that answer those questions, or you can read the book from cover to cover. Really, you can read it while you stand on your head if you want to (and if you're good enough at standing on your head!). While you're reading, if you find anything that doesn't make sense to you or makes you feel weird or scared or that you have questions about, ask your mom or dad or find another adult you can talk things over with.

There's one thing you should know about adults, though. Even though they've been through puberty already that doesn't mean they are comfortable with the subject. Just like you, adults may be a little scared about talking about all this stuff. You could try using this book as a starting point in your conversation. Sometimes just having something in your hands makes getting a conversation going much easier. Also, this is just one little book so we can't possibly answer every question you have. That's why you'll find additional resources in the Resources section in the back of this book.

While this time may pose some challenges for you, you already have many resources for dealing with the changes that are coming your way. You have people who love you and want to help you make sense of things. You have friends who are experiencing the same things you are and can understand what you're going through. You have past experiences that you've learned from, and you have your own ideas and hopes and dreams to look forward to. All these things will help make the next few years easier for you. Best of luck to you as you begin the journey that will take you from a girl to a woman. You can do it!

THE EXPERT SAYS

It is very important to get accurate information about the changes that occur in puberty, so talking to an adult is the way to go. Your friends may have lots of information, but often it will be wrong.

CHAPTER 1

In the Beginning: A Quick Intro to Puberty

Feeling confused about all the changes going on inside (and outside) your body? You're not alone. Whether you've already experienced some of the changes in your body that are described in this book, or whether you are at the very beginning of this process, having the right information about what is happening in your body can make this time easier and perhaps just a teensy weensy bit less stressful. Puberty happens whether you feel ready for it or not, but as your teachers have probably already told you many (many) times, knowledge is power. Knowing in advance what will be happening in your body can help you get ready for what's ahead. Surprises might be good for birthdays, but they're no fun when you're talking about puberty's big changes.

Ah, there's that word again. Puberty. It's possible you've been wondering what this "puberty" is that your parents, teachers, and friends are talking about, and what on earth it has to do with you.

Know the Facts

Some girls start puberty as early as eight years old, but other girls start much later. Developing earlier or later than your friends doesn't make you weird; puberty is a very individual process, and your body develops when it's ready.

Here's the scoop: puberty is the name of the process that your body goes through when it makes the transition from kid to adult. There is growth and change—a lot of it—some of which can be seen from the outside, and some that just happens inside. Often when girls think of puberty or growing older, or what adults call "becoming a woman" they think of getting their menstrual period. But while starting your period is one obvious sign of puberty, there's a lot more to it than that.

The changes of puberty begin with some action from the pituitary gland. The pituitary gland—which is located just under the base of your brain, in case you were wondering—sends a chemical message to two small glands called the ovaries. In response, your ovaries begin to grow and produce another substance, a hormone called estrogen.

How's The Air Up There?

Almost always, the first sign of the newly released estrogen doing its work in your body is a growth spurt. Your hands and feet grow first usually, then you will grow taller, your hips will get wider, and your waist will get smaller. Usually the growth spurt slows down a little about the time you start your first period. But most girls do still grow an inch or two after their first period.

Hey! There's A Breast On My Chest!

A bit later—probably during the middle of your growth spurt—you will start the very first stages of breast development. In the beginning of this process you will develop something known as breast "buds." These are small mounds that form under the nipple and area of darker skin around your nipple (known as the areola).

THE EXPERT SAYS

As you get older, your doctor will usually reserve some time at every check-up to talk to you alone. This is a good time to ask any questions you might have about your changing body – especially about things that might seem embarrassing.

MR. LAMONTE'S
6th GRADE CLASS

It's common for one breast to start growing before the other. It's also common for your breast buds to hurt a tiny bit in the beginning, but as your breasts start becoming rounder and more full, this tenderness should go away. Read more about breasts in Chapter 3.

Is That A Hair Down There?

Yes, it probably is. About the time breast development starts, most girls begin to grow pubic hair (hair near and around the vagina). There might not be much hair at first, and it might be straight and very fine. You might also start to grow hair under your arms, or that might happen a bit later. Some girls don't grow underarm hair until the very end of puberty.

And One More Thing....

You might start to notice a light yellow or white stain on your underwear. This is called vaginal discharge. Vaginal discharge is a normal part of the way your body cleans itself. Vaginal discharge is just one more reason why you need to change your underwear every day.

Know the Facts

Most girls have their first period about a year after their first vaginal discharge, and about two and half years after they first start to develop breasts.

Life is either a daring adventure or nothing.
HELEN KELLER

CHAPTER 2

Taking Care of Business: Your Changing Body and All Its Bits

What do you think of when you think about growing up? Getting your period? Growing breasts? Learning to drive a car? All these things are important parts of growing up and we'll talk about them in a bit (well, except for the driving the car part; you'll have to go to drivers' education for that) but they aren't the only things affected by this wild and wonderful process called puberty. In this chapter you'll find some information on how to take care of your body's rapidly changing parts, from top to bottom, head to toe.

Your combs, brushes, and other hair care items get dirty just like your hair does. Wash them with shampoo and warm water at least once a week.

If you think you can, you're right; and if you think you can't, you're right.
MARY KAY ASH

Starting At The Top: The Hair On Your Head

Hair care can be a little bit complex for girls because there are so many choices of hairstyles to choose from. Still, the basics are the same whether your hair says "high style" or "short and simple."

❋ **Lather. Rinse. Repeat.** As you get further into puberty, you might find that your hair is more oily than it used to be. That's those pesky hormones at work again! If you are very active, or your hair is particularly oily, you might need to wash your hair every day.

❋ **Use hair care products made specifically for your type of hair.** Different hair textures, especially, need different grooming products. Check labels or ask for help at the drug store. The place where you get your hair cut might have suggestions too, but keep in mind that products bought in the hair salon are almost always more expensive than products bought anywhere else.

❋ **Hair can't take the heat.** Chemical processes (like perms, either to straighten or to curl, or coloring), and processes where you apply a lot of heat to your hair (like

blow-drying) damage your hair and make it harder to take care of it in the long term. The less you use these processes, the less special conditioning products you will need.

❋ **Every night should be a wash out.** Hair styling products can be fun, but what you use during the day should be washed out before you go to bed. This is especially true of wax-based products, such as certain types of gels. Shampooing out styling products before you hit the sack gives your hair a break from being covered in goop and keeps you from waking up with hair that looks like something from a horror movie.

Hair In New Places

Growing hair under your arms and on your legs is a part of growing up. There is no medical reason to remove this hair and women in many cultures don't even consider it. However, if you think you

Some deodorants can leave marks on your clothing. The marks are particularly noticeable on dark-colored clothing and when you are wearing tank tops or spaghetti straps. To cut down on these marks look for deodorants that say they dry "invisible."

would be more comfortable without the hair, talk with your mom or another adult at home about the best way to get rid of it. The most common way to do this is by shaving, but there are other ways of getting rid of unwanted hair. Ask an adult for more information if you need it.

Other Underarm Thoughts

You may have noticed that you are a little stinkier under your arms than you used to be; or if you haven't noticed, your older brothers and sisters might have decided to inform you. This again, is a part of the puberty process. Frequent bathing helps a lot. You can buy special deodorant soap to use on the particularly smelly parts of your body, but try to use a milder soap on the other areas (your arms and legs, for example) because deodorant soap can be very drying.

You'll also want to start experimenting with different types and brands of deodorant until you find one that works best with your body chemistry. Avoid antiperspirants. These actually stop you from sweating, which you don't want. Sweating is a natural body process that helps you cool off.

Shaving Your Legs: A Beginners Guide

So you've noticed some hair on your legs and you want to get rid of it. Here are some tips to help your first shave go a bit smoother (no pun intended).

1. Hop in the shower. Don't ever shave dry legs. The heat and moisture from your shower will help your shave go much smoother and help you avoid cuts and nicks.

2. Don't feel like you have to spend more on shaving cream aimed at women. Shaving cream is shaving cream. Using shaving cream does make shaving go easier though, so try to use it.

3. Use a new razor and replace your razor regularly. Old razors won't cut the hair but they may cut you.

4. Start at your ankles and shave up.

5. Put some lotion or moisturizer on your legs after you are done. This will keep your skin from getting dry.

Ears So Dear

If you ask your doctor or nurse practitioner, I bet they will say the most important thing you can do for your ears is not to stick things in them! Pen caps, paper clips, even cotton-tipped swabs can all really hurt your ears if you stick them in too deep. Washing your hair regularly should keep your ears clean, but it doesn't hurt to scrub lightly on your outer ears with a washcloth. Make sure you get behind your ears, where dirt can easily collect. Especially if you have short hair, it can show to other people even though you might never see it!

You know that wax you have in your ears? You might think it's a little gross sometimes, but it has a very important function: it keeps dirt from getting further down into your ear where it can do real damage. So make peace with your ear wax and let it do its job. Feel like your ears are clogged or having trouble hearing? Have a chat with your health care provider about things you can do to help get rid of some of the wax.

Eye See

What are those two things in between your ears? Oh, wait, they're your eyes. I'm sure we don't need to tell you how important your eyes are to you. You use them every day. The main thing to remember with your eyes is that if you are having trouble seeing, you need to tell your parents so you can get your eyes checked. Some people have trouble seeing things that are close to them. These people are far-sighted. Most people who have trouble seeing, though, are near-sighted, meaning they can see things that are close to them, but have trouble seeing the blackboard and other things that are further away.

If you do have trouble seeing you'll probably end up getting glasses. Lots of people have them. While they might be difficult to deal with at first, you'll get used to them. After you've had glasses a while, you might look into getting contact lenses. Talk to your parents to figure out if contacts are right for you.

Facing Your Face

When you're in the midst of puberty, your face can be the focus of a lot of worry and concern because of one word: acne, also known as pimples, or even "zits."

Almost no one gets through puberty without a few pimples on their face, but knowing that doesn't make it any easier when they

Notes from a Real Girl:

On adjusting to having glasses:
At first it can be annoying to have them on. That was true when I first got them, like when I was playing sports, or doing something else outside. If you just got glasses and you're getting teased, ignore it. I know that's hard to do but soon enough everyone will get used to your new look.

If you do get a pimple, don't pick at it or (and this is very tempting) pop it. This just irritates the skin more and can cause a deeper infection, which can cause a permanent scar.

start popping up for you. Pimples start when excess oil becomes trapped in your pores and combines with bacteria (i.e. germs) and dead skin cells. You can't entirely prevent acne. The extra oil on your skin is part of the (yes, you guessed it) gift of the changing hormones in your body, but there are some things you can do to help your skin look and feel better.

❄ Whether you have acne or not, you should be washing your face once a day. Washing does not mean scrubbing—you're a girl, not a kitchen pot. Use a gentle, non-scented soap and warm water. And try not to touch your face, because touching your face helps spread germs and can lead to more breakouts.

❄ If you have more than an occasional pimple problem, you might be tempted to try the many products that promise to zap the "zit monster." The most common and effective treatments that you can get without a prescription contain benzoyl peroxide. You can buy these at the drugstore. Follow the directions carefully though, and don't use more than the label says. Benzoyl peroxide can be very irritating if you use too much.

❄ If the over-the-counter products don't help, talk with your parents about visiting a dermatologist, a doctor who specializes in the treatment of problems of the skin.

Notes
from a Real Girl:

On the best way to deal with pimples:
Just keep washing your face and don't pick at them!

Keeping Your Teeth From Giving You Grief

It might be that by this time, no one is standing over you making you brush your teeth. Your parents might already trust you to do a good job with this bit of personal hygiene. You probably already know quite a bit about how to take care of your teeth, so this is just a quick review of some important mouth care facts:

❄ Look for a toothbrush that has soft bristles. A toothbrush that has hard bristles can actually make tiny abrasions in your gums and lead to more problems! Replace your toothbrush every three to four months. The bristles get worn out after that and can't really get your teeth clean.

❄ Don't forget to brush all the surfaces of your teeth: outside (the sides touching your cheeks) and inside, as well as the flat surfaces. You should brush your tongue too, because bacteria can hide there and lead to very smelly breath!

❄ Remember, in order to get your teeth really clean, you need to brush them for 2 to 3 minutes, which is a longer time than you might think. Using the timer on a microwave can be a good way to find out if you're brushing long enough.

❄ Finally, floss floss floss! Flossing removes food bits and bacteria from in between your teeth, helps avoid cavities, and keeps your gums strong. If winding the floss around your fingers is too clumsy for you, you can buy single-use floss picks that are small pieces of plastic with the floss already attached. They are not cheap, but they make flossing much easier.

The secret of getting ahead is getting started.
SALLY BERGER

Going To The Dentist

There is a lot you can do to make your teeth healthier at home, but there are some things (like filling a cavity) that can only be done at the dentist's office. Even though not all families have health insurance and not all health insurance plans cover going to the dentist, there might be ways people (especially kids) can still get good dental care. Talk to your school nurse for some ideas about how the adults in your life can make this happen.

A lot of people (not just kids) don't like going to the dentist. If this is true for you, make sure you ask lots of questions about what is going to happen at the dentist's office. We're not saying that having all the information is going to make your trip to the dentist's office like a fun trip to the zoo. But the more information you have, the better prepared you will be for what will happen.

Of course, for girls who need braces, there can be even more trips to a special type of dentist, called an orthodontist. If you are one of those girls, don't despair. Braces can be a short term pain in the mouth for a long term gain. Teeth that are straighter and lined up better within your jaw (the two most common reasons for braces) are easier to clean, and having straighter teeth can lead to a healthier mouth overall. Also, the better care you take of your braces—avoiding foods that are hard on the brackets and bands, being extra careful with brushing—the shorter the time you will have to wear them.

Keeping Your Feet Neat

Although you might not think about your feet as body parts that need much care, they do some of the hardest work for you so it's worth taking a look at what they might need to function best.

First of all, feet need good supportive shoes that fit properly. And even though you might be absolutely desperate to wear them, especially as you get older, there are very few varieties of high heels that provide your feet good support. High heels can cause blisters, hammer toes, and bunions, not to mention leg and back problems! If high heels are a "must have" in your wardrobe, make sure you get shoes that have some room near the toes. Shoes built with a suitable "toe box" are not as hard on your feet as those that crush your toes into a point. Also, save the high heels for special occasions where you won't have to wear them for more than a few hours at a time.

A very common foot problem that almost everyone gets sometime in their life is called "athlete's foot." Athlete's foot is spread in places that are dark and damp and where people go barefoot. Sounds like the locker room, right? This is why it's called "athlete's foot." Athlete's foot is a kind of fungus, but you can prevent it by wearing flip-flops (keep special ones just for this purpose so they don't have outside germs on them) or shower shoes in public showering areas. If you notice itching and peeling on your feet, especially around and in between your toes, you might have athlete's foot. It's easy to treat with anti-fungal sprays or powders you can buy at the grocery or drug store.

Feet are not the sweetest smelling parts of our bodies, but there are simple and easy things to do to make your feet smell less yucky. Washing your feet is important, of course, but it's also important to always wear socks with your shoes. You'll want to air out your shoes between wearings, too. You'll notice some shoes get stinkier than others: shoes that are made out of non-breathable materials like plastic make your feet sweat more. Make sure you wash your feet every day, and dry them well, especially in between your toes.

A strong, positive self-image is the best possible preparation for success.
JOYCE BROTHERS

CHAPTER 3

The Care and Feeding of Your Body (Part Two)

In the last chapter we talked about your ears and toes, and everything (well, okay, not everything) in between. You might be saying, "Hey, I know that isn't all there is to know about what's happening in my body during puberty. What about, you know, the really girly stuff?"

We're so glad you asked. We saved all the "girly" stuff, the stuff that just happens with girls' bodies, for this chapter. Hopefully, a lot of your questions about what's going on "down there" and "up here" (meaning your chest) will be answered right here!

Breasts—When Are They Coming? (Part 2)

Some girls eagerly await breast development, and go to sleep with visions of training bras dancing in their heads. Other girls might feel like they got busty too early and even feel awkward around other (less developed) girls their age. But despite these feelings—and it can be difficult to get breasts before or after most people your age—there really is a lot of variation to what is considered normal. Some girls' breasts start developing when they are just nine years old. Other girls might not develop breasts until they are almost 14!

Having breasts that develop later—or earlier—than the rest of your friends might feel a bit embarrassing (who wants to be different than the rest of the kids in your class?) but it will—we promise you—ultimately be okay.

Many girls will start to have breast growth within one year of the time the girl's mother had her first breast development. This is only a rough guess, though, since different factors like nutrition, health, and exercise can all influence hormone levels and therefore breast development.

Here are some more important breast facts:

❋ You might have one breast that develops slightly faster than the other breast. This is normal and will most likely never be noticed by anyone but you.

❋ No one size or shape of breast is healthier than any other size or shape. Having bigger or smaller breasts doesn't make it harder or easier to breastfeed or increase or decrease your chances of developing breast cancer.

❋ Sometimes breasts that develop very quickly will have stretch marks that look like spokes going around the outermost part of the breast. Even if these marks are a little noticeable now, they will lighten with time.

❋ Although most experts don't recommend regular breast self-examination for several years yet, it's still important to become familiar with the way your breasts look and feel. This will help you be aware of any changes later on.

Supporting Your Breasts—Bras And Beyond

Once your breasts start developing, the question that girls often wonder about is, "When do I need a bra?" Wearing a bra is mostly a matter of comfort. Some girls like the feeling of support a bra gives them, especially when playing sports or running and jumping. There is no harm in wearing a bra earlier rather than later, but you'll probably need to convince your parents (especially your mom) that it's the right time for you.

You'll want to take your mom, an older sister, or another female adult on your first bra-shopping expedition. Before you go, there are some things that it's helpful to know.

First, there are different types of bras. The first bra a girl usually has is a training bra, which doesn't provide a lot of support, but does help you get accustomed to wearing a bra. Some girls find bra-wearing itchy at first, so it's best if a training bra doesn't have much lace or frills to annoy you. As you get bigger, you might be interested in other types of bras, including some that have wires (covered of course) to help give some structure to the bra

There are two ways of spreading light: to be the candle or to be the mirror that reflects it.

EDITH WHARTON

and therefore more support to you. A sports bra (sometimes called a "jogbra") is another kind of bra that provides even more support. Sports bras usually fit more snugly. You don't have to be into sports to wear a sports bra; some girls like how they look and feel and wear them all the time.

Sports bras are sometimes sized simply as small, medium, and large but other bras are sized with both a chest size (in the US this is measured in inches) and a cup size. The cup size is measured from AA (smallest) to EE (largest).

Progressing To Your Period

What is commonly called "getting your period" is also known as beginning menstruation. In the simplest terms, menstruation is when a small amount of blood comes out of your vagina over a few days. Although this might sound a little scary, it's a normal process that happens every month to women, starting during puberty and continuing until the age when they can no longer have children.

In order to understand why this happens, we'll need to do a little anatomy review. Girls are born with a place for babies

QUICK TIP

The best way to figure out your bra size is to go to a store that specializes in bras. The store will usually have someone called a "lingerie specialist" (which is a fancy way of saying "bra fitter") who has experience in helping women find bras that fit. She will measure you and help you pick out a bra that fits best, supports you, and looks good under your clothes.

to hang out and grow until they are ready to come into the world. This place is called the uterus. Not too far from the uterus are two glands called the ovaries. The job of the ovaries is to produce female hormones and also to store the eggs that could one day develop into a baby.

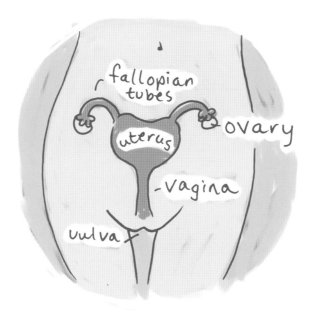

Starting in puberty, about once a month, your ovaries release one of these eggs. The egg travels down a special egg highway (also known as the fallopian tube) that leads from the ovaries to the uterus. This process takes about three days. During the time before the egg reaches the uterus, the lining of the uterus (also known as the endometrium) thickens, by filling up with blood and fluids. If the egg is fertilized (connects with a sperm to make the very beginning of a baby) the thickened lining is a nice cozy spot for the fertilized egg to grow into a baby. If the egg arrives in the uterus and is not fertilized, the uterus doesn't need the extra lining it has built up, and it releases the blood and tissue through the vagina over a period of a few days.

Your First Period– How Will You Know?

When you get your period for the first time, you might feel a small amount of liquid coming out of your vagina. Sometimes it's hard to recognize this feeling in the beginning; it's more likely that you will first see something red or rusty/brown on your underwear.

Your first period can be a little surprising even if you know it's coming. (One reason for books like this is so girls won't be surprised.) But there is no need to panic. Your period won't start flowing heavily all at once, so you have time to get some supplies. If you're away from home and don't have anything with you, you can ask the school nurse (that is, if you're at school) or the mother or grandmother of one of your friends.

The items used to soak up menstrual fluid are called sanitary products, or sometimes, "products for sanitary protection." You are probably familiar with disposable pads and tampons (and see the next page for some pros and cons of each), but there are also some other items (like washable pads) that are not as hard on the environment and might be safer for girls and women to use. You can read more about them on some of the websites listed in the Resource section.

Some girls tell all their friends when they get their period. Some girls tell just a best friend. Some girls choose to keep it mostly private and maybe only tell their mom and sisters. You should do whatever makes you feel most comfortable. Remember it's your personal information; you don't have to share it with anyone, even if they ask. And no one can tell by looking at you that you've started your period.

During the first few years of having your period, you might feel like it is an exclamation point! Your first periods might be irregular, might start and stop, and might get off track when you're stressed out or not feeling well. This is common, but by the end of the first year or two of menstruating, most girls will have regular periods.

Know the Facts
Pads vs. Tampons

Here's a comparison between pads and tampons which may help you figure out which is right for you.

Where Do They Go:
Tampons: **Inserted inside the vagina. Although this may sound gross or difficult to do, most girls get used to it after a few tries. Once a tampon is properly inserted you can't even tell it is there.**
Pads: **Attach to your underwear. This is easy to do (and no one will know it is there) but you may notice a bit of an odor if you don't use deodorant pads.**

How Often Do You Have To Change Them:
Tampons: **Depends on how heavy your flow is, but figure every 3 to 4 hours. Be sure to change your tampon at least every 6 hours. Never sleep in a tampon.**

Pads: **Depends on how heavy your flow is and how large a pad you used, but figure every 3 to 4 hours. There are "overnight" pads that are meant to be worn longer, but you won't want to wear these during the day because they can be somewhat uncomfortable.**

What About Sports:
Tampons: **Girls who wear tampons often have an easier time participating in sports. Yes, you can go swimming while wearing a tampon.**
Pads: **Except for swimming, play away. Today's pads are often so thin that you forget that they are there.**

Ask your mom or health care provider for more information about pads and tampons. You might also want to try them both to see which is right for you.

Your menstrual cycle (this is counted as the time from the first day of one period to the first day of the next period) will usually be between 21 and 35 days; the average is 28 days. A woman's period can typically last from one to seven days. Keeping track of your period on a calendar will help you remember when your period is likely to happen.

This Period Is A Pain: PMS And Cramps

Getting your period is a normal part of healthy body functioning. You aren't sick when you have your period, and there is no reason to change your daily activities. You can swim, play sports, and do anything else you would normally do, as long as you're comfortable.

Some girls do get cramps that come with their period. These cramps are caused by your uterus contracting as the blood flows out of it. Sometimes girls also get pain in their abdomen or back, and nausea, or even a little bit of diarrhea. One of the best treatments for menstrual cramps is heat; either from a warm bath or a heating pad. Exercise can help with cramps during your period too, as does drinking lots of fluids. Over-the-counter pain medications such as ibuprofen can help you continue your daily routine. If pain relievers don't help, you should contact a health care provider to see if the cramps are more than just normal period cramps .

During the time of the month right before your period starts, you may have something called premenstrual syndrome (PMS). PMS is caused by changes in your hormones. Some girls get more moody during this time. They might feel irritable or might cry more easily. They might also find they have a craving for certain foods.

Being generally as healthy as possible is the best defense against PMS. Getting some exercise and avoiding caffeine also helps. As for the mood swings, one of the easiest things to do is keep track of your periods on a calendar. Then you'll know when you are due for your period, so if you find yourself crying for absolutely no reason at all, you can at least remember, "Hey, nothing weird is happening here, I've just got PMS."

THE EXPERT SAYS

The hormonal changes that come with getting your period and getting it regulated can make you feel like you're on an emotional roller coaster. But as your periods become more regular and you continue to get older and more mature, the emotional side effects usually settle down.

Your First Visit to Your Gynecologist

Going to the doctor who specializes in the stuff "down there" can be a nerve-wracking experience for a young girl. It's probably been a few years since anyone but your mom (if even your mom!) has seen you naked. Here's a brief guide to what you might experience at your first exam.

1. The nurse will show you into an examination room and after taking your medical history (asking about your periods and stuff like that) she'll tell you what items of clothing to remove. Usually she'll give you a sheet to cover yourself with so you'll never be totally naked. If you'd like your mom or another friend to come with you, just ask. Most places don't have a problem with this.

2. The table for female examinations often has stirrups at the end of it. These are for you to place your feet in while the doctor examines your vagina and female organs. They may look a bit strange but the stirrups make it more comfortable for you during the exam.

3. The doctor will first examine the outside parts of your vagina and make sure everything has developed normally and is okay. The doctor may then see if it is possible to insert a device (called a speculum) that makes it possible to see inside the vagina. The doctor may also place one or two fingers

inside your vagina and one hand on your abdomen. This allows the doctor to feel your ovaries and your uterus. The doctor is looking to examine them, and to make sure they are normal size and have developed appropriately.

Don't hesitate to ask questions or to hold your mom's hand. Yes, it can be a difficult few minutes but hang in there and give yourself a treat (a nice bubblebath always works well) when you get home. The good news is that you probably won't have to go back to this doctor for another whole year.

CHAPTER 4

Your Health and Your Body

Did you know the most important thing you can do for your rapidly changing body is to love it? Every day we are bombarded with images of what a woman should look like from commercials on TV, magazine covers, and billboards. But most of the women in those pictures have spent literally hours getting ready for the picture to be taken. They have teams of people to apply make-up and do their hair. And even after all that, once the pictures are taken, anything that doesn't look "perfect" is fixed by manipulating the photo itself.

THE EXPERT SAYS

Separate who you are from how you look. Your personality matters much more in the long run than facial features, body shape, or fashion.

So the point is, your physical body will probably not look like the pictures you see in a magazine, because the person in the magazine doesn't even actually look like her own picture! Our bodies are very diverse and wonderful and come in all different shapes and sizes. Comparing your body to someone else's body will never make you happy and will not make you healthy either. Taking care of your body, and loving your body for what it is and what you can do with it, on the other hand, will help you be happier and healthier.

Girls And Food

Girls as young as six or seven sometimes talk about "being fat" or needing to "go on a diet." And while it's important to make good food and movement choices so our bodies can run well and we can do things that give us joy, dieting is a bad idea, especially for young girls. Here are just a few reasons why:

❈ Young girls need good nutrition and calories to keep growing.

❈ Dieting makes food the enemy. Food is fuel and it should be fun. Learning to make good choices can be part of the fun.

❈ Because a diet usually has a list of "good" and "bad" foods, dieting makes it harder to listen to what your body really wants.

❈ Most fad diets require that you give up entire categories of food. This makes it very unlikely that your body will get the nutrients it needs.

Dieting isn't a good idea, but learning about nutrition is. You probably have some ideas about what good nutrition is all about, but for more details check out some of the websites listed in the resource section.

Learning what to eat is important, but so is learning how to eat. For example:

❈ Work with your body. Your body sends you signals that say "I'm hungry," and it's important to be able to know what these feel like. When you are eating because you are upset or bored instead of hungry, it's harder to make healthy food choices.

❈ Make food choices based on how you feel after you eat certain foods. Do you have more energy? Do you feel tired? Restless? Queasy?

❈ If you are looking to get away from junk food, try different foods that might especially interest your taste buds. Try foods from another culture, or foods that are flavored with different ingredients than you are used to.

❈ Although fresh fruit is a tasty and convenient snack, sometimes girls get bored with the old "apple in the lunch" routine. Ask your parents if you can try different kinds of fresh fruit, and remember fruit is best when it is in season (meaning close to the time it was picked). You might have learned this when you tried a supposedly fresh tomato in the middle of the winter only to find it didn't taste much better than cardboard. If your family can afford it, try organic fruit, it has an even better flavor.

❈ Don't get discouraged if you are trying to eat more healthily and fall back into old patterns. It takes time to change habits. If you keep listening to your body and keep trying to make choices that will give you energy, you'll find yourself eating well.

Healthy Eating For Girls On The Go

If you've got a busy schedule it can seem like a lot of work to try to eat healthy food. Here are some tricks that may help guide you to the types of food that will keep you healthy while satisfying your tastebuds.

❄ Always carry a piece of fruit with you. Stick with hard fruits like apples and oranges. Softer ones like pears and bananas will turn into a mushy soup-like substance in your backpack in no time. In the winter months, there is nothing like the sweet taste of a clementine to wake up your taste buds, and since it comes with its own wrapping (also known as the peel), you can just grab it and go when you are on the run.

❄ Think about "healthier" choices instead of "good" or "bad" foods. You can't always get organic kale and steamed chicken breasts for dinner, and even if you could, you'd get bored fast. Instead, when

you can't get the healthiest thing, look for food that is less processed and has fewer additives. For example, if you only have access to a vending machine for an afterschool snack, you might not be able to get baby carrots. But you could probably find pretzels or another food that's not fried and maybe has some nutritious content.

❊ Here's another great tip: carry nuts in a small bag with you at all times. Nuts last even longer than fruit, are less messy to eat, and have protein. They'll also keep you full a long time!

Worried About Weight

Even though it's much healthier (and much more fun!) to think in terms of healthy eating and healthy movement choices rather than diets and exercise, girls are under a lot of pressure to be slender and many girls are very afraid of the "F" word: fat.

Television and movies don't do a good job in showing girls the range of healthy body types that are out there. If you only get your body image from the media, you might think that every girl is tall and slender. Not true! Girls come in all different shapes and sizes and the trick is to find and accept the most healthy size and weight for your body type.

If you're worried about your weight, take a minute and think about what you are really scared of. Are you worried that you will be unhealthy? Are you worried that boys won't like you? Are you worried that you'll be teased? Ask your parents to help you figure out if what you're worried about is likely to happen and if it does happen, what your options are. You can also talk with a health professional (like a doctor or nurse practitioner) about whether your weight is right for you.

Get Moving!

Little kids naturally move around a lot. However, once kids go to school and have to start sitting still more than six hours a day, they slow down. Often the only time kids get time to jump and run around is at a very short recess. Then, to make it worse, as kids get older, organized sports become a more and more important part of outside play and physical education. Sometimes kids who aren't Joe or Janet Jock stop enjoying moving their bodies and become more sedentary. This is not healthy and it's definitely not fun.

Even if you're not a basketball superstar, there are lots of ways you can make physical activity a part of your life. You can:

❄ Try individual sports, or sports that don't require a whole team to participate, like running or tennis.

❄ Experiment with activities that you might enjoy but that aren't competitive. Yoga is a good example. No one loses at yoga!

❄ Go for walks. There's a whole world out there to explore, even without leaving your neighborhood.

❄ Go for hikes (hikes are basically walks where there are lots of trees).

✻ Relearn active games you might remember from when you were younger, like Twister or Red Rover or kickball. You might want to stay away from dodgeball, which too often causes hurt feelings and worse!

✻ Suggest social activities with your friends that involve physical activity. Maybe go for a bike ride together or go in-line skating.

✻ Go swimming on a hot day. If you haven't been moving in a while, swimming is an especially good choice because it's easy on your joints!

✻ Go to the mall. Yes, that's right, the mall. Walking around the mall can be good exercise. Some malls even open early to give walkers a safe place to get moving.

You can probably come up with even more fun ways to get your body moving if you think about it. Remember, people come in all different weights and heights and sizes and shapes. If you can develop loving habits that take care of your body now while you're still young you will be healthier—and much happier—as you grow up.

Girls And Sports

If you like sports, team sports can be a great way to help you keep fit, spend time with friends, and enjoy what your body can do!

Being great at a sport can be really fun, but you don't have to be the best on the team, or even be on the winning team, to enjoy yourself. Some reasons to play a team sport:

✻ Release stress and pent up energy from sitting still all day. (It's hard to worry about your math homework when you're trying to hit a fast ball!).

THE EXPERT SAYS
About Eating Disorders

There are two main types of eating disorders. If a girl has anorexia nervosa, she will intentionally starve herself. If she has bulimia, she will eat huge amounts of food and then force herself to get rid of (purge) the food from her system. Both types of eating disorders are very serious conditions and require the girl to get professional help to live a healthy, active, happy life.

Eating disorders typically begin around the time a girl starts puberty and can last her whole life if not treated. Here are some signs to watch for in yourself and your friends. If you think you or someone you know has a problem, remember, help is out there. Talk to an adult or see the resource list at the end of the book for more information.

Anorexia Nervosa:

Girls with anorexia nervosa:

- Are often convinced that they are fat. Although they may be "as thin as a rail" or "a stick figure" to other people, when they look in the mirror they see someone who is overweight.
- May be obsessed with food. They may talk about it constantly and even cook huge meals, but not eat the food themselves.
- Are usually obsessed with exercise. They may work out for hours to get rid of any calories they may have eaten.

Bulimia:

It may be more difficult to tell if a girl has bulimia because her body weight will often stay around the "normal" range.

However, here are some things to watch for:

Girls with bulimia:

✷ Are very body and weight conscious and are frequently dieting. They think a lot about body weight and shape and use it to raise or lower their self-esteem.

✷ Eat an excessive amount of food during a short period of time and feel a lack of control over how much they eat. They often feel like they cannot stop eating until all the food is gone.

✷ May force themselves to vomit or use other methods to prevent weight gain from the large amounts of food they've eaten.

Treatment for bulimia and anorexia nervosa include therapy with a trained psychologist, medication, and sometimes hospitalization. Remember, help is out there. Sometimes the hardest step is just asking for it.

QUICK TIP

Try not to judge yourself based on how other girls your age look. Just because your best friend is ready to wear a bra, that doesn't mean you should wear one. And just because four girls you know have their period, that doesn't mean there is anything wrong with you if you don't. Every girl develops at her own pace. Eventually, every girl ends up with the shape she is supposed to have.

❋ Have fun.

❋ Get exercise and enjoy what your body can do.

❋ Learn skills (like how to pass and dribble, but also self-confidence, self-discipline, and teamwork).

❋ Make friends.

Team sports can be especially good for girls because they can help you keep your body confidence as you go through puberty. Sports can be a good way to ensure that you still do the things you enjoy even if you might feel a little bit awkward about the way you move in your always changing body.

Sometimes adults push kids too hard in sports. While pushing yourself a little can be good, pushing yourself and your growing body too much can lead to permanent injuries. If you are feeling so much pressure that sports have lost some of their fun for you, it might be time to talk to your parents about this.

Keeping Healthy Self-Esteem During Body Changes

Many girls find all the changes coming their way confusing; some worry that if they don't change at the same time—or in the same way—as other kids, they will have to put up with a lot of teasing. We know that it can sometimes be difficult to be seen as different from the kids around you, but everyone's body develops when it's ready.

It helps to have someone to talk these things over with, hopefully someone who can remember her puberty days! It can also be good to discuss things with friends. And there are books like this one, as well as internet sites, where you can find lots of helpful information

about your changing body and your changing life. It's important to remember, however, that you are the expert on your own life. No one can know you, and your body, like you do. This special time in your life is a great time to learn to listen to yourself and to your body and pay special attention to what it has to say.

Notes from a Real Girl:

On finding a good adult to talk things over with:

Try your mom first, but you can also talk to your sister, auntie, or even your dad!

CHAPTER 5

Changing You, Changing Home

Many girls, no matter what their family situation, say that as they enter their late pre-teen years, life at home gets a whole lot more, well, "interesting" is one way to say it! It's natural for your friends to become more important to you as you get older, this is an important part of growing up. At the same time, figuring out how to still get along with your family, even though things are changing, is a very important skill. Remember: you can make a difference in your life at home!

Help! My Mom Is Driving Me Crazy!

You may have noticed that as you've gotten closer to puberty, you have more conflict with your parents, or the people who serve as parents for you, whether they are foster parents, grandparents,

or your aunt. Sometimes this conflict is around certain issues like after-school activities, curfews, school-work, video games, or TV watching. Sometimes it might seem like the conflict comes out of nowhere and you find that your parents can annoy you just by walking into the room!

This is certainly no fun, but it is completely normal. The job of kids as they get older is to separate from their parents until they are independent enough to live on their own. The job of parents is to give kids loving guidance, set limits, and make sure they are actually ready to live on their own when the time comes.

So while kids and parents mostly have the same goal (for the kid to be ready to be an adult when the time comes), kids and adults don't always agree about how to get to this goal. That's where the conflict comes in. No matter how unreasonable your parents' actions might seem to you (and, of course, some parents are more reasonable than others), you can't control them. You can control your own actions, though, and sometimes this can help make things a little smoother around the house. Here are some tips for maintaining a good relationship with your parents:

✳ **Keep talking.** If you explain something once and your parents look at you like you're an alien dropped from a spaceship into their living room, it's easy to clam up, give up, and go to your room. But try giving your parents another chance. Explain again what you're feeling and what you want from them, maybe using different words. Ask what part they DID understand and start from there. Your parents may never "get" everything about you, but if you give up sharing too early, you might miss the support they do have to offer.

✳ **Keep listening.** Many families have a "no slammed doors" rule. But when you refuse to listen to anything your parents are saying because you don't agree, it's just like slamming a door. Even if the conversation continues verbally, you don't come any closer to an agreement.

Spend time with your family doing things together. Parents are going to be more okay with you spending time with your friends if they know you make family time a priority.

Remember, it's not just words that can hurt feelings. Ever had a friend frown at you when you first arrived at school in the morning? It hurts, doesn't it? If you continually roll your eyes, make a face, or frown at your parents, they are going to have a reaction and you are probably not going to like it.

Learn how to "fight fair." Girls are going to have conflict with parents, there is simply no way around that. But some conflict can be positive, if tempers are kept under control and certain guidelines are observed. For example, avoid name-calling. If you're in the middle of a discussion that is turning into an argument, ask to take a break and calm down, and don't be afraid to apologize if you hurt someone's feelings.

Pick your battles. You don't care about everything equally, so try to give in without a big discussion on some things you care less about. Your parents will listen more closely when you bring up an issue if they don't feel like you are always complaining about every rule they make.

Negotiation: "Please?" Is Not Enough

In order to successfully negotiate with the folks who are the "boss of you" at home, it helps to have some basic understanding of what they want and need.

For example, one of the most common areas of girl/parent conflicts is curfew. You think you're old enough to stay out really, really late and your parents want you back in the house as soon as the sun goes down.

Despite what it might feel like sometimes, most parents don't set a curfew based on what they think will make you the most miserable or will most effectively ruin your entire social life. They probably have concerns either about your safety or about you getting enough sleep for the next day's activities. So it's important to ask your parents what their specific concern is and listen to their answer.

THE EXPERT SAYS

Most parents really DO want to give you more privileges as you grow older; however, you have to show them that you are mature and responsible enough to handle the privileges. Ways to show that you are responsible include things like completing your chores without complaint, doing your homework in a timely fashion, and being honest and upfront with them, including "owning up" when you mess up.

For your negotiation with them to be successful, you'll have to address their concerns. For example, if your parents know that you are at a safe, supervised, age-appropriate activity, they are going to be much more likely to be flexible about your curfew. Sharing more information about what you are doing and where you are going—even if you think it's boring to talk about these things with your parents—might calm their fears a bit. Brainstorm ways to communicate with them about what's going on and reassure them that you are safe. Try to be open to ideas that they suggest and find a way to work together to get to your common goals.

Parents will be more likely to be flexible about curfews if you show them that you have good judgment and a good plan. For example, talk with them about what you would do if you were at a party

It's nice to be important, but it's important to be nice.
MELISSA HAHN

and realized there was drinking going on, or your ride home disappeared.

Your parents will not be able to give you a lot of freedom unless you have made it obvious to them that you can handle some freedom. Show them how seriously you take your responsibilities and your part of the agreement. For example, the first time you are out after you have agreed on a later curfew, come in ten minutes before you are required to be in.

A final note about negotiation: don't ask for exceptions to rules at the last minute or in front of your friends. A private conversation is going to go better in most cases, because your parents won't feel pressured by the audience.

QUICK TIP

Offer to text your parents when you arrive at—and leave from—a party or move from one activity to another. This will keep them in the loop without missing a moment of fun.

Notes
from a Real Girl:

On negotiating with parents about curfews:
Ask directly and smile. Be respectful and have good reasoning. Your parents should be impressed with the fact that you put so much thought into it.

Do Your Chores Before You Fly Out The Door: Negotiating Work At Home

Most families have expectations about how kids help out. This might include small things like clearing the table after dinner, or bigger things like housecleaning, or even helping with a family farm or store.

These expectations can be a source of conflict between girls and parents, especially if girls feel like helping around the house cuts into their social time too much. There are some ways to (you knew this was coming, right?) negotiate about chores so that both parents and girls will feel like they are getting some of their needs met.

Goals are dreams with deadlines.

DIANA HUNT

If you and your parents are feeling frustrated around the subject of chores, ask for a family meeting to discuss things. Prepare for the meeting beforehand by thinking about what areas need to change and what compromises seem reasonable to you. It might help to come armed with some additional areas of chores that you might be willing to do to help the house run smoothly

in exchange for having less responsibilities in another area. For example, if helping with dinner puts too much pressure on you to get home quickly after sports practice, maybe you could ask what you could help with in the morning instead.

If your parents complain that you are not doing a good job at the chores you are doing, ask for more details about exactly what they expect to be done. Try making an actual list: break the chore down to its smallest parts and check each of them off as you do them.

Notes *from a Real Girl:*

On doing chores:
Even though I don't particularly like doing chores, I make them more fun by competing with my siblings to see who can get them done first.

Do I Really Have To Live With These People? Getting Along With Brothers And Sisters

Siblings can be absolutely infuriating! You may get angry if they take something that is yours, go into your room without asking, or bother you when you have friends over. Your older brothers or sisters may try to boss you around and tell you what to do. Your younger brothers or sisters may borrow your things or want to be around you all the time when you just need a break and want to be left alone.

One of the most difficult things about sibling arguments is that they happen in a close space. When you argue with your friends, you can go home and get away from them. But when you argue with a brother or sister, they are in your house and you may feel like you can NEVER get away from them!

Here are some ways to make and keep sibling peace:

❈ Go for a walk or go to separate rooms in the house before you lose your temper in an argument.

✳ If the same argument keeps happening, talk to your parents about what is bothering you. Most likely they will be able to give you some advice.

✳ Set up your own personal space. Even if you share a bedroom, set aside a little place (even in a corner of your bedroom) that is all yours. Make sure you respect your brother or sister's personal space too, whether it is their room or a part of your shared bedroom. If you do this, they will be more likely to show you the same courtesy.

✳ Don't do things that break down your relationship with your sisters and brothers. This includes physical violence (hitting, throwing things) but also name-calling, breaking promises, telling secrets, and not respecting property and personal boundaries.

✳ Work to build your relationship with your siblings. Try and think of shared projects you can do together that will make happy memories, like working together on a scrapbook of your family vacation, or cleaning out the basement to make a cool, new hang-out spot.

Notes from a Real Girl:

On the best way to make peace with your siblings: Find something nice to do for your sibling that's unrelated to your fighting, that usually works.

CHAPTER 6

The Ever Growing Outside World: School, Friends, and Feelings

Okay, we've covered some important topics: your body, your family, lots of things about your new changing life. But we haven't talked about some of the people and places where you spend a lot of time (friends, school) and the feelings that affect your daily life. Not to worry, we've got you covered in this chapter right here.

Off To School You Go

Do you remember your first day of kindergarten? You might have been worried about not being able to get to the bathroom in time, missing home a lot, or not having much success with scissors. Now that you've successfully dealt with all those challenges, it might be just the tiniest bit frustrating to find that each year in school brings with it new and improved things to worry about!

It's true that school life for girls in the older elementary grades or middle school can be difficult in some ways. But exciting things are happening too. You probably have a little bit more freedom, like being able to choose a few of your classes or even teachers. You might even have more fun classes that give you opportunities to do things like learn to play an instrument. Plus you might have new chances to hang out with other students, learn things together, develop some of your talents, and even find some new talents you didn't even know you had!

> *If you want to stand out, don't be different, be outstanding.*
> MEREDITH WEST

Grades

Most kids—even the very best students, for whom schoolwork comes really easily—worry about grades sometimes. You've probably had to adjust your thinking about grades as you've gotten older, since this is just about the time many schools change from the satisfactory/not satisfactory way of grading (or something like it) to giving actual letter (A, B, C, D) grades.

It might seem like the whole concept of grades is an evil plan to give adults and kids one more thing to fight about. But what grades are really supposed to measure is how much you've learned. That's one big reason parents want their kids to earn good grades: they want to know that kids are learning something at school. But grades are only one way to measure how much you've learned, and they aren't a perfect way.

Grades only measure a specific kind of intelligence. So if you are a girl who struggles with schoolwork, or has to work really hard to get the kind of grades other students seem to get easily, it does not mean you are not smart. Did you hear that? Struggling with schoolwork does not make anyone "dumb" and don't let anyone tell you that it does. If school is not that easy for you, you can bet that you have special skills somewhere else, even if you haven't discovered them yet.

Studying: It's A Skill!

Although some girls are naturally better students than others, all girls can improve their work in school by having good study habits. The skills you need to be a good student are called (not surprisingly) "study skills," and there are entire books, classes, and websites designed to teach kids how to develop them. But even without reading an entire book, there are some simple steps you can take to improve the way you study.

1. The most important study skill is to know what you're supposed to be studying. That's why a small assignment notebook or calendar is something that can be really helpful. Maybe writing down all the assignments you've been given and then crossing them off when you're done doesn't exactly sound like rocket science, but it's a really easy first step to better schoolwork. Using a "to do" list lets you use your brainpower to do the algebra problems instead of trying to remember which ones you are supposed to do!

2. One way to prepare for class is to engage your brain even before the class starts. As you are getting out your work, or walking into the room, coax yourself to think about the subject you're about to study instead of wondering whether anyone is noticing that you are having a very bad hair day. You might be thinking, "Ugh, it's bad enough to think about math while math class is going on!" Still, if you are mentally prepared for what's

ahead, you'll be able to follow along right away instead of missing important information while you are switching gears.

3. Be an active listener. Paying real attention in class is different than listening to your i-pod or watching TV. While the teacher talks, think about how the information fits in with what you've already learned, or how it could be used in your daily life. In some classes, you might need to take notes; this can be a great way to keep your mind on track!

4. If you are having trouble concentrating on your studies, use a timer (you can use a cooking timer or the clock on the microwave) to help you develop your "stick-to-it" skills. Hate spelling? Promise yourself to do nothing but study your spelling words for 25 minutes, then set the timer. When it goes off, get up and take a five minute break and then head back for another round of study. When you've finished studying, reward yourself with some downtime or a favorite TV show.

5. Take extra care to get enough sleep and eat breakfast during the school week. If there are difficulties at home that make it hard for you to do these things, it might be helpful to talk with your parents about the situation, or mention it to your teacher or guidance counselor.

6. Develop a study routine: a certain place you always study, where you have all the materials you need (extra paper, pens, etc). Unless you really must use the computer for the assignment, choose a spot far away from the internet. Watching one more YouTube video of someone who taught their dog how to use a yo-yo is always going to seem more interesting than algebra.

7. Don't make schoolwork more stressful by putting it off until the last possible minute. A lot of times we procrastinate because a task seems overwhelming. If this is true for you, try to break the assignment into smaller parts and then work on one part at a time.

Notes *from a Real Girl:*

On studying:
Make time to do it even if you don't want to, and remind yourself that if you study harder, you'll get a better grade eventually.

"I Can't Believe I Got Miss Crabapple!" Dealing With Difficult Teachers

Some teachers you will meet during your school career will be amazing. You might feel like they care about you, or feel like they really "get" you. That kind of situation usually makes learning easier, even if it isn't always fun.

On the other hand, sooner or later you are going to run into a teacher who you have a harder time with. It might feel like the teacher doesn't like you, doesn't understand you, or is too strict. While it's normal to have some teachers you like and some you don't, if your relationship with your teacher is making it hard for you to learn, there are some things you can do to improve the situation.

✻ Since you can only change your own behavior, look at that first. Do you show up on time? Do you do your homework? Are you respectful? Do you ask questions when you don't understand something? If you answered no to any of these questions, look to changing your own behavior first.

❖ If your teacher has some "pet peeves" (behaviors that particularly annoy or bother them) getting along might be as simple as not doing those things!

❖ If you need to bring up an issue with a teacher, do it after class. Most teachers are more relaxed one-on-one than when they are dealing with a whole classroom of kids.

❖ Sometimes it might feel like the problem is the teacher, when the real difficulty is that the subject they teach is one you don't like or that you have a hard time with. If the class is hard for you, make sure the teacher knows you are doing your best.

❖ Talk to your parents about the problem. They can help you set up a meeting with the teacher where you can talk about the problem.

QUICK TIP

If you really dislike a subject, ask a classmate who seems to like it why she enjoys it. This might give you a whole new way of looking at science as well as a whole new way of looking at that science-loving girl who sits in front of you!

If you can't change your fate, change your attitude.

AMY TAN

Finally, in a situation like this it's important to understand that even if you don't connect easily with your teacher, it is not necessarily someone's fault. You are going to like some teachers better than other teachers, just like you like some people better than others. It might not be fun, but you can learn valuable skills about getting along once you learn that you don't have to actually like a teacher to learn from them.

Keeping The Fun Stuff Fun: Extra-Curricular Activities And You

In general, the older you get, the more different types of organized after-and-before school activities there are for you to get involved in. These activities might be offered through school or through a community organization like a local recreational center, library, or church. These activities can be great opportunities to learn new things, practice skills, meet new kids, and learn how to work as a group.

It's important to remember that even though you are still a kid (or between a kid and an adult), your time is precious. If you are involved with an optional activity, it should be because you are enjoying it. Of course, any activity you're involved in is going to have some aspects that aren't that much fun. No one expects you to be jumping up and down in excitement, for example, about running laps to get ready for basketball season. And you might prefer not to attend all those extra practices that the chorus has when it gets close to the time for the winter concert. But if you don't get any joy out of being on the basketball team or hate everything about being in the chorus, you might want to consider dropping it.

Here are some tips to make your extra-curricular activities extra special.

❉ Be safe. You can't have fun if you're getting hurt. Wear protective equipment (this applies to sports mostly. If you need protective equipment when you're writing for the school newspaper, something has gone really wrong!), warm up before beginning anything that requires strenuous physical movement, follow the safety rules for whatever activity you're doing, and stop immediately and tell the adult in charge if you are injured.

❉ Mix it up. Involve yourself in some activities that are physically active, and some that require more brain power than muscle power. This is the time to be trying lots of different activities, find out what you like.

❉ Don't take things too seriously. Involvement in outside organized activities can be a really great way to develop self-discipline and learn how to do your best even when you don't feel like it. However, if you are too intensely focused on achievement and winning instead of just having fun, you miss a lot of the experience. There are plenty of places where life puts pressure on you, don't add to it!

❋ Honor your schoolwork. Teachers say that after-school jobs especially, can contribute to kids getting lower grades and being super tired in school. If you really want to work as you get older, it's best for your schoolwork to pick jobs where you can decide when to work (like babysitting) or to work very limited hours (like on the weekends or only one or two evenings a week).

❋ Use extra-curricular activities to explore career choices, but don't be in a rush to decide. If you think you want to be a doctor or a nurse, it might be great for you to volunteer at your local hospital when you get old enough. The real-life experience might be enough to tell you, "Wow, this is exactly what I love," or "Man, I really can't stand the smell of hospitals one bit!" At the same time, just because you couldn't handle hospital smells at 13, it doesn't mean you won't be fine with them by the time you go to college. You have plenty of time to grow and explore.

❋ When looking for activities to try, think outside the popularity box. You don't have to be good at sports and cheerleading to make good friends. How about joining the school newspaper, taking pictures for the yearbook, running for student government, or even playing chess on the chess team?

❋   Build some "down time" in your life. Just hanging out with your friends is an important part of growing up. Everyone—adolescents especially—need time to be relaxed without the pressure of some structured activity.

You have the power. You are the magic wand.
LAURA SCHLESSINGER

Friendship Skills

If a supportive group of friends is one of the things that will help you get through middle school (and well, life in general) it's probably worth spending some time really thinking about what qualities you look for in a friend. You might want to consider which of these qualities are most important to you:

❋   If they say they are going to do something, they do it, even if it is inconvenient for them.

❋   Can keep a secret. How many times has your grandmother told you, "If someone talks about someone else to you, when you're gone they'll talk about you to someone else?" Well, unfortunately, it's very true.

❀ Will be there for you even in hard times.

❀ Doesn't pressure you to do things you don't want to do (things that go against your personal values or beliefs).

❀ Is easy to talk to/gives a feeling of comfort.

❀ Is a good listener.

❀ Makes time for you.

❀ Is predictable. No one is in exactly the same frame of mind all the time, but it's much nicer to be around someone who is able to control their moodiness.

❀ Has a good sense of humor (makes fun of themselves or life, not of you).

As you read over this list, and add some thoughts of your own, you might notice that these may not be traits that all the kids in the "popular" clique at school really have. Having friends—and being a good friend—is different from the middle school concept of popularity.

Once you know what you are looking for in a friend, it becomes easier to find people who you will "click with," rather than "be in a clique with." Look around at school (don't forget about the boys, too!) for kids with these characteristics, but don't stop there. You can make friends on a community sports league, through your family, in your neighborhood, or pretty much any place kids gather!

THE EXPERT SAYS

Be friendly to kids you meet even if they appear not to be. Smile and say hello! These gestures will help you to make friends faster because friendly people are likeable people.

Dating And Romance

Sometimes girls wonder if the rules for talking to boys change now that they are older. Boys are (believe it or not) people and so the best way to talk with them is to use the same great people skills you use with your friends who are girls. That means having conversations that go beyond a quick, "What's up?" when you see a boy you know in the hallway. Instead, take a moment to ask how the big game was, what he got for his birthday, or how his dog is doing. You may soon find that he's asking you the same sorts of questions, and before long it won't seem at all strange to talk to a boy. He'll be a friend just like any of your other friends.

Sometimes friends and siblings pressure close friends who seem like they could be romantically involved to call what they are doing "dating" or "going together." This can be hard on a friendship since if you're dating you can easily break up and lose the friendship, while if you are just friends this is much less likely to happen. Don't put pressure on yourself to call any of your close friendships "dating." Just move at the speed that comes naturally to you and enjoy getting to know lots of different people.

On having boys for friends:

It's actually very normal to have a boy for a friend or even a best friend. One plus side is that they don't gossip as much, unlike girls, who (sometimes) can sit around and talk all day.

If you feel a lot of pressure from your friends to jump into dating before you are ready, it can help to make at least a few friends who are running at your same speed when it comes to romantic

Making new friends might seem really difficult if you are naturally shy, but if you learn how to be a good listener you can often make friends without always being the one to make the first move. Smiling and asking open ended, non-personal questions are also good ways to keep a conversation going.

relationships. You can also ask your friends to back off a little bit. Let them know that you'll try dating when you are ready.

Dress For Success

Your parents are probably starting to give you a little more choice about what kind of clothes you want to wear and you're probably even starting to develop your own personal style. It can be really fun to experiment with different fashions and see what looks best on you. There are a lot of different types of fashion out there and that means every girl should be able to find a style that suits her. For example, some girls are fashionistas. That means they like the latest styles and trends. Some girls are casual, opting for jeans and t-shirts every day. Some are more conservative, aiming to look stylish but in a more adult manner, and some girls never get out of their sweatpants, even for fancy occasions. Each of these fashion choices is great, although keep in mind that there are a few fashion pit-falls you should be aware of.

Fashion Pitfall #1: Even though you see a lot of pictures in magazines and images on television of young girls wearing really tight and really skimpy clothes, you'll probably want to wait until you're older to decide if those kind of styles are right for you. Those kind of styles attract attention that's really more appropriate for adults, and it can be stressful to deal with that kind of attention all the time. If you wear clothes that are a little looser and cover a little bit more, people will tend to think of you as someone who has a lot of self-respect. And that's a very, very important part of being grown up!

Fashion Pitfall #2: Sweats are really comfortable, we get that. However, there is a time and place for everything, and while lounging on the couch is great for your favorite PJs, the school dance might not be. If comfort is your thing, look around for fancier clothes that still allow you to move freely. For example, a tight dress with stockings and high heels might not do it for you, but a soft sweater with a comfy skirt and high boots might dress you up without stressing out your comfort zone.

Fashion Pitfall #3: If you are one of those girls who has 5 pairs of the exact same jeans and 5 t-shirts that are alike except that they come in different colors, then your fashion pitfall may be that you haven't taken the time to experiment with fashion. While it's okay to wear jeans and t-shirts most days (see Fashion Pitfall #2), why not see if you also like skirts, dresses, or pants that don't come in denim? You might discover that you have a love of flirty skirts, a flair for ruffle pants, or enjoy the powerful feeling that comes from wearing more business-oriented type clothing.

Get A Job!

A part time job can be a really great way to learn responsibility by earning some of your own money to pay for things you want or need. You might not be able to get a regular job working at a store or a restaurant until you are over 16, but you can probably earn some money running errands for a neighbor, babysitting for kids you know, or mowing lawns. A job can be a great learning experience and can expose you to careers you may not have considered before. Just be careful that your job doesn't interfere with your schoolwork or with getting enough sleep!

Spending Vs. Saving

Once you've earned some money, you should go out and spend it, right? Not so fast. Part of growing up is thinking about the future. Ask your parents for their advice and assistance about putting money away for your future and for saving for smaller items like special clothes or special activities that you wouldn't otherwise be able to buy or participate in. You may want to start a savings account of your own so you can be even more active in saving up for the things you'll want and need as you get older.

Looking Forward

Even if you're just old enough to start babysitting and you haven't even started thinking about what job or career you'd like to have when you grow up, it can still be fun to learn about the different possibilities. If you have a career you're interested in, you might be able to volunteer around that type of job and see what it's really like. You can also read books about that career or research it online.

But no matter what career seems interesting to you right now, keep your eyes and ears open for new possibilities. Your interests are likely to change over the next few years and so will your ideal career choice.

CHAPTER 7

Staying Safe in the Real and Virtual Worlds

The internet is amazing! It helps us connect with friends and family, research school projects, learn about hobbies and interests, and keeps us entertained. The internet is not dangerous by itself, but some of the people who spend time on it and some of the situations that can happen are dangerous, so it's important to take some steps to keep yourself safe.

The most important thing to remember about the internet and electronic communication (like texting) is nothing is really private. Never post anything online, or send anything in an email or a text message that you wouldn't want the whole world to know. That means the whole world: your best friend, your worst enemy, your teacher, your principal, your mom,

your grandma...everybody. The way electronic communication works, it's easy to forward personal photos, information, or videos. But it's almost impossible to get the photos or information back once they're out there!

Think of an electronic form of communication as a big billboard on a highway near your house. If you wouldn't want it appearing on the billboard, don't text it or email it to anyone. Also, don't post it on your Facebook page, on tumblr, or twitter or any other way of communicating electronically.

Also remember that on the internet, almost everyone is a stranger. And your parents have warned you about talking to strangers, right? Make sure your parents or another adult know if someone you don't know (even if they say they are a kid) contacts you in a chatroom or on email. And never, ever (get it, ever!) agree to meet someone you met on the internet in person without your parent's consent.

Finally, be aware that a lot of not so nice things go on among pre-teens and teens in the virtual world. From "Beauty Pageants" where friends vote on each other's looks to cyber-bullying that makes kids feel like outcasts, it's easy to get caught up in the seedy underside of social networking. But you have the power to change this. Be a force of good in your cyber community. Instead of participating in demeaning contests or contributing to a rant that is bound to hurt someone's feelings, fill your cyberspace with love, respect, and peace.

Cliques And Mean Girls

"Sticks and stones may break my bones,
but words will never hurt me."
-Something parents sometimes say,
and girls know is NOT true.

Does it seem like you just woke up one morning to suddenly find a group called "the popular kids" that never existed before? The end of elementary school and the beginning of middle school is about the time when groups of kids often start breaking off into cliques.

Some "grouping off" is to be expected at this age, as girls band together with other kids that have similar interests. A group of friends that travels as a pack because the kids in the group have things they like to do in common (like collect comic books or skateboard) might not really be a true clique. The thing that makes cliques dangerous is when some kids in a clique refuse to allow other kids to be a part of an activity, especially if there is bullying and teasing involved.

It is a rare girl that can make it through to high school without suffering some hard days because of bullying and teasing. A very important thing to remember is that when cliques exist only to keep certain girls out, they are not about socializing and friendship anymore. They are about power and control. Everyone feels insecure at this age. Kids who run the meanest cliques are usually the kids who feel the most insecure and are trying to make themselves feel better by keeping other kids down.

Not that knowing this really helps, right? Especially when adults give you advice like "just ignore it, they will stop teasing you if they see it doesn't bother you," which might be true (maybe, eventually) but is really hard to do when you are stuck at the bus stop for 20 minutes with someone who just made up thirteen different rhyming ways to insult you.

The cruelty of girls to one another is something that scientists (really, it's true) have gotten involved in studying. They have figured out two things that help protect girls from the effects of being teased: not blaming themselves for what they are being teased about, and having a supportive group of friends.

Peer Pressure: Pushing Back

Part of what makes bullying and the "mean girls" so effective is how powerful peer pressure can be. Pressure from peers doesn't always look like the typical scene from a corny movie made by adults where kids sit around in a circle and tell each other, "C'mon, everyone is doing it." Peer pressure can be very subtle. A lot of decisions you make every day might be influenced by information you get from your peers and things you see them do. For example, think about how you made the decision to put on the clothes you have on right now. Hopefully wanting to be comfortable was a part of your decision, but there were probably lots of other thoughts too, including what your friends would think!

This is why adults are always bugging, er…reminding, you how important it is to choose your friends very carefully. The way your friends act, talk, dress, study (or don't study) all have the potential to influence the way you act, talk, dress…well, you get the picture.

So obviously choosing your "peers" carefully is the first step in making sure peer pressure isn't a negative thing in your life. There are also other steps you can take to help push back against peer pressure, for example:

✻ If you are anticipating a situation in which you might be under a lot of peer pressure to do something you don't want to do, brainstorm ways you can deal with it. You might even want to ask someone to role play with you to get some practice!

✻ Keep it together. Try not to get caught alone. If you know it's hard for you to say "no" to cutting class with a bunch of other students from your grade, talk with another friend who might be feeling pressure about this. Agree to be each other's peer pressure buddy (you can probably think of a cooler way to say it) to help resist the temptation.

✻ You don't have to give a detailed answer for every decision you make. Sometimes just saying, "No thanks" and nothing more can be a powerful way of communicating that the conversation is over.

✻ If you are having trouble saying "no" remind yourself what you are saying "yes" to. For example, saying no to a cigarette is saying yes to nice breath and healthy lungs.

✻ Finally, remember even adults have peer pressure, so learning how to manage it now might be hard, but it will pay off big both for your future and in the future.

QUICK TIP

The best way to not get sucked into blaming yourself for getting picked on is to concentrate on all your good qualities and really value yourself as a person. Finding and developing your talents and skills can help with this a lot; so can learning to talk to yourself and about yourself in a positive way.

Bullying And Teasing: How To Protect Yourself

Sometimes cliques and mean girls go beyond just being annoying and their behavior becomes straight up bullying. You are being bullied if other kids at school are saying and doing things that make you feel unsafe, either emotionally or physically. Bullying can take many forms. It can be someone sending you mean text messages. It can be someone threatening to beat you up. It can even be some so-called friends asking you to do things that you know you shouldn't do. If this happens, the first thing you should do is tell an adult you trust.

If that adult doesn't help you, tell another adult. If that adult can't help, ask someone else. It might be hard, but you have to believe that you are worth the effort and that you don't deserve to feel scared at school, in your community, or at home.

In addition to asking an adult for help, try to build some support with your friends. Don't keep what's happening to you a secret. If a kid or a group of kids are bullying you, you can bet they are bullying other kids as well. Maybe you can start an anti-bullying club where you make sure every kid in your class has someone to walk home with, or maybe you can start a "safe" table in the cafeteria that allows anyone who wants to sit there to sit down. If these ideas don't apply to your situation, figure out what does. And remember, you are not alone. By giving your family and friends a chance to help you, you are allowing them the opportunity to show you how much they love and care for you.

Personal Safety

It's not fun to listen to grown-ups talk on and on about how dangerous everything is. Let's be real girls: not everything in the world is dangerous, and certainly not everyone in the world is out to do something bad to kids. However, in order to feel safe and secure, you need to develop certain skills to help you recognize safe and unsafe behavior and you need to have good boundaries between yourself and the rest of the world.

For example, you should have already been taught that your body is your own, and no one has the right to touch you in a way that makes you uncomfortable or scares you. No one, except for sometimes a doctor in a doctor's office, should touch you anywhere in your private areas, which are the areas usually covered by a bathing suit. Even if that person is someone your family knows, or a relative, or someone who is very nice to you or pays special attention to you: they still don't have the right to touch you in these areas. If someone does try to touch you in a way that doesn't feel right to you, it's not your fault. It's never your fault when an adult doesn't respect your private areas, even if they say it is. If this happens to you, you need to tell your parents or another adult you trust as soon as possible.

There are things you can do out in the world that will help maintain your boundaries. For example, of course you shouldn't talk with strangers, or get into a car with someone you don't know well, or accept gifts from adults you don't know. You should also make sure not to give any personal information about yourself to people who don't need that information. This includes information you may give out electronically, for example by filling out entry forms for contests or posting personal information online.

If you are home alone after school or while your parents are at work, it's best not to broadcast this fact. Always ask to see the badge or identification card of anyone like a police officer or a gas repair person who comes to the door. Always check with your parents to see if they are expecting them before you open the door; you can even check the badge through the peephole, that's what it is made for! When in doubt, don't open the door. Just tell whoever it is to come back again some other time.

CHAPTER 8

Stressed Is Desserts Spelled Backwards

Stress is a part of life. You're never going to get rid of it, so you need to decide how you are going to handle the particular things that stress you out. Different girls react to stress in different ways, just like different girls get stressed out by different things. For example, it may not bother you that the date of the school carnival was moved back by one week, but your best friend might see this as a major stress-out situation and start freaking out.

There is a funny saying that you might see on people's Facebook wall or even on t-shirts: Keep Calm and Carry On. It's actually a great way to think about stress. First of all, don't panic. Take the time to adjust to the new situation, to see the good, the bad, and the different, and then make choices based on what seems best for you. If the problem seems too big to handle yourself, don't handle it yourself. That's what adults are for. Get them involved and you're likely to cut your stress level significantly.

Different Bodies, Different Brains

Just like different kids get stressed out by different things, some kids bodies may need different accommodations to help them be the best they can be. One example of this is medication prescribed by a doctor. Some kids need medication to keep their bodies working properly and some need medication to help their brains work properly. Many times, girls with ADHD (Attention Deficit Hyperactivity Disorder) might need to take medication of some kind in order to be able to sit still in school, focus, and finish their work. If you're one of these girls, it's important to remember there's not something wrong with you or your brain, your brain just works a little differently than some other kids' brains.

Sometimes kids have brains that make it hard for them to understand what people mean when they say things, or to understand how friendships and conversations work. Sometimes kids who have brains that work in this specific way are said to be on the Autism Spectrum. They might take medication or they might need to be told things in a certain way, or they might need to be in a classroom that is run in a way that helps their brain work best.

There are lots of ways a girl's body might work a little differently than other kids in her class. Some girls, instead of walking, use a wheelchair to get around. Some girls might wear a hearing aid or need special glasses.

These differences don't have to be stressful. When they are, it's usually because people in the bigger world haven't spent any time thinking about how they can make sure their part of the world is accessible. For example, if a girl who uses a wheelchair has a house with a ramp, she might not really be stressed out by using a wheelchair. That is, until she arrives at her new middle school and finds there is a flight of stairs and no elevator to her home room. Clearly it's not the wheelchair stressing her out, it's the lack of thinking by the people at her school that causes the stress.

If you're a girl who has encountered some of the stresses from the world not working the way your body or brain works, keep reminding yourself it's not your fault. You will probably have to keep finding ways to work around your difficulties because no one cares as much about your success as you do. Just remember, the problem is not you, your body, or your brain.

At some point, you are likely to have a class or ride the bus or be in a community group with another girl who has a body or brain that might not work like yours. It's normal to feel a little uncertain about how to treat that girl. There is no one right way to interact because each girl is an individual and each situation is different. If you think the girl might want some help with something, ask if you can help, and make sure you listen closely to her answer. You probably know this already, but ignoring or teasing kids who are different than you won't make either you or them feel better. Every person has feelings. Every girl wants to have friends and be liked. You might find that if you go a little bit out of your way to befriend a kid whose brain or body works "different", that it's you who will gain the most from the friendship.

Moving

Moving can be one of the most stressful experiences in a girl's life. There are a lot of things that are hard about it, like:

✽ Leaving your old neighborhood.

✽ Getting used to a new house and a new room.

✽ Making new friends. This can be especially difficult if you are moving in the middle of the school year.

✽ Missing old friends.

✽ Missing your daily routine where you lived before you moved.

✽ Being ahead or behind in classes because your old school taught different things than your new school teaches.

Believe it or not, there are some positive things that can come out of moving. What? Well, for example:

✽ An opportunity to make new friends.

✽ Getting closer to siblings, since they are the first "built in" friends you have at the new place.

QUICK TIP

To get yourself excited about the move, think about how you will decorate your new room. If your old room still shows a lot of the little girl you once were, take this opportunity to make your new room represent your personality now.

When you look for good things in life, you are much more likely to find them.
LAURÉ KENDRICK

✳ A chance to start over in a new neighborhood where people don't know you, and build your reputation from the ground up.

✳ Learning new skills, like how to make friends, and how to find out what you need to know about a new area.

When your parents first tell you about the move, you might be really mad. So for a while you might not be ready to talk to them about it. But when you are, ask questions. A good first question is, "Why do we need to move?" If you ask after you have had a chance to calm down and let the news sink in, you might be able to understand the answer. You might not like it, but you will eventually be able to accept the move better if you can see it is something your family needs to do.

Take the lead on going online and getting the information you most want about your new area. What is most important to you? A softball team? Ballet school? A place to hike or a safe playground? Your new school probably has a webpage where you can see what it looks like and what kind of extra-curricular activities they offer. Use a web-based satellite map feature (like Google Maps) to see what your actual neighborhood looks like.

If you are going to move at the beginning of the summer, ask if you can join a team, go to camp, or find some other way to meet people before school starts. This will give you a head start on meeting friends so it won't be such a lonely summer for you and a scary new school year come fall.

Divorce

The first thing all girls need to know about this subject is simply: divorce is not your fault.

Divorce is about two grown-ups and the way they get along (or can't get along), not about the kids in the family. If your parents get divorced (or even were never really together in the first place), it doesn't have anything to do with you. You can't cause your parents' divorce by behaving really, really, really badly. And you can't prevent their divorce by behaving really, really well.

When you first hear that your parents are splitting up, it might seem like your whole world is turning upside down. You might have many changes to adjust to all at once and you might feel torn between your parents, or like you have to choose sides. Although some of this will get better with time and everyone getting more used to the new situation, you can ask your parents for some help in dealing with the divorce.

✳ Ask your parents to communicate directly with one another rather than using you as a messenger service.

✳ Ask for advance notice about changes in custody arrangements or where you will be going when and who you will be with on holidays and birthdays. Sometimes last minute adjustments have to be made, but the more information you have, the more secure you will feel.

✳ Ask your parents not to vent about the other parent to you, or around you.

Divorce is usually hard, especially at first. But you might find there are some things that are better about the new situation. Although it can be stressful to split your time between two homes, it can be even more stressful to live in a home with constant fighting.

Drugs, Alcohol, And Other Unhealthy Stuff

Are you looking at this section and thinking "why is this stuff in here? I'm way too young to be worried about alcohol and drugs?"

Hopefully, you are, but it's not true for all young people. In fact, six percent of all kids your age say they drink alcohol on a regular basis.

You might not have a lot of people in your life smoking, drinking alcohol or using drugs, but even if you don't, you still get exposed to tons of advertising for alcohol and tobacco products. One of the ways ads try to get kids interested in tobacco is by showing smoking as a "grown up" or adult thing to do. As you face the difficulties of growing up it can be tempting to create a false sense of being grown up by smoking, drinking, or getting high.

But facing your problems head on and being present instead of numbed out by illegal substances is the best way to prove to yourself and the people around you how grown up you are.

If you are going through a hard time, it can be tempting to drink and get high in order to get a little break from your

THE EXPERT SAYS

There is almost always someone, usually a caring adult, who will be able to help you when you need it. Remember that, even if that adult is not in your own home, he/she is out there somewhere and wants to help you grow up into a healthy, happy young woman.

problems. Unfortunately, this just makes your problems get bigger; if you're feeling sad and get drunk, your brain has a harder time recovering from your sadness and depression. Not only that, all the trouble that getting drunk causes just piles on more problems.

Remember that prescription drugs, if they aren't prescribed to you, are still very much illegal and can do just as much damage to a growing brain and body as anything that comes from the streets!

The best place to get information about drugs and alcohol is from your parents. They especially need to know if someone is asking you to try drugs and alcohol. It can be especially hard to say "no thanks" if there are lots of drugs around you. If this is true, talk with an adult you trust to see if there is anything you can change in your environment (like where you live, where you go to school, and what adults you are around) to help you stay away from drugs. Even if you can't do something big like move or change schools, maybe making some small changes, like finding a different way to walk to school, could help.

Super-Stressed Families

Every family has stress, but some families have much more stress to deal with than others. For example, some families have to cope with homelessness, having very little (or no) money, someone in the family drinking too much or using drugs, or living in a neighborhood with a lot of crime.

Sometimes (not always) situations like this make it hard for the adults in the family to be consistent, even if they are trying very hard. Sometimes these adults might need some help so that they can be the kind of parents they want to be.

If you are afraid of someone in your family, or aren't getting your basic needs (clothing, food, going to the doctor) met, or your family is super-stressed in some way, it's very important that you talk to someone. Your school guidance counselor or the school nurse are usually good people to start with. It might be really hard to ask for help, but it is very brave. Kids from stressed out families do NOT have to be messed up.

Also, if one of your friends is in a super-stressful situation at home, talk to a grown-up you trust about getting them some help.

Handling Stressful Situations

Even if you're not in a super-stressed family situation, you can still have a lot of stress in your life and you might need help from the adults closest to you to come up with coping strategies and tools to help you deal with stress and stressful situations.

One way to change the way you react to stress is to change the way you think about things. For example, sometimes we might look at a situation and only see the bad when there is some good in the situation. Or we might think that because we feel a certain way, the way we feel must actually reflect reality. Or we see things as either all good or all bad, even though most situations are some of both. Ask a good friend or an adult who is close to you to help you see some of the ways your thinking might be causing you stress.

> The one thing that doesn't abide by majority rule is a person's conscience.
> HARPER LEE

Another very powerful way to keep stress from getting the best of you is to always be thinking about a bigger goal or something you are working for in the long term. For example, let's say you're a girl who cares a lot about animals and you have the goal of helping five puppies from a local shelter get adopted. If you went out to start putting up signs to tell people about the puppies and it suddenly started raining, you might be annoyed about the rain. But you probably wouldn't be as stressed out about it as you would be if you weren't so concerned about the puppies. The bigger goal would help you not be as stressed about the little things you can't control.

Stress And Your Friends

Part of being a good friend is helping your friends through their stressful times. One of the best ways to do this is by being a good listener, especially a good listener who can hear a friend's problems without giving a lot of advice.

You can also help your friends deal with their stress by offering to assist them with tasks that might be overwhelming them. For example, if your friend's parents get divorced and she has to pick some clothes to be at her dad's house and some to be at her mom's house, she might feel like this task is really, really big. You could offer to come help her do that chore. Even just hanging out, even if you can't

There is nothing better than the encouragement of a good friend.
KATHERINE HATHAWAY

actually do much to help, is still a great way to help your friends with their stress.

Just as your friends should expect you to be there for them during stressful times, you should expect the same things from your friends. If you need help, call them. If they need help, be there. Together you will make it through all the challenging times that growing up can dish out.

Be The Boss Of Your Feelings

With your body and what seems like your whole life changing more every day, it can be easy to get overwhelmed with very strong feelings. It's really important to remember that feelings are not right or wrong, they just are. For example, it's not bad to feel angry about something. The fact that you are feeling angry tells you something

about the situation or yourself. It might mean you need to work on changing the situation (if you can). Or you might need to work on how you view the situation, if you don't want to continue to feel angry. The problem with strong feelings only comes when we act on the feelings in a way that hurts ourselves or others.

Here's an example: if your little brother "borrows" your toothbrush to spread the glue on his model cars, it would be very normal to feel angry. In the moment, you might want to use his toothbrush to clean the bathroom floor. But we are sure you can see why talking to your parents about the problem might work out better for everyone involved.

Of course, in order to make the better decision in cases where you are having strong feelings, you need a way to get rid of some of the big physical and emotional energy that comes from them. Then you'll be able to act instead of react.

Notes
from a Real Girl:

On what you should do if you have a fight with a friend:
Do not say mean things about her to any of your other friends. Even though you think it will make you feel better, trust me, you will regret it.

A common way for girls to work out strong feelings is to talk to a friend. Did you know you can help your friends be better listeners by communicating what kind of support you need from them? For example, if you want your friend to be really paying attention to what you're saying but she seems distracted, try saying, "I have something that I really want to talk to you about. Would you mind if we put down the video games for now and just really talked?" Or if you have a friend who always gives advice when you would rather they just listen, you can say, "I really appreciate that you want to help me out, but right now I really just need to vent." And if you do want advice, you can also ask directly!

You can also write out your feelings. Whether it's a notebook stuck under your mattress, a password protected file on your computer, or a special leather-bound book with a padlock built in (yes, they do make those), a journal can be a great way to express yourself. Not only can journaling take an edge off of some of the strongest feelings and help you calm down before making a decision, it's an awesome tool because you can go back and read over what you've been through in the past. And if you can get someone to walk with you and listen to your feelings, you'll be pretty much guaranteed to boost your mood.

Physical activity is also a great way to work out your feelings. A fast walk can not only get you out of the situation for a few minutes but you might also feel a lot better when you come back!

In Conclusion

You've grown a lot already, probably even since you started reading this book. But you still have even more growing to do. While growing up may be difficult at times, keep in mind that you only have to go through the process of puberty once in your lifetime. Remember also that all the experiences of growing up—the good, the bad, the happy, the sad—are what will make you into the person you are meant to be. Finally, know this: there is no one perfect way to be a girl! Some girls like roses and pink princess t-shirts and some girls think pink princess t-shirts are the worst. Some girls like to play the drums on a drill team and some girls like to play the flute. Some girls never want to get dirty. Some girls think getting dirty is the best. None of these ways to be a girl is wrong!

Respect the girl you are inside and say good things to yourself. You're on your way to being a strong, amazing woman, so don't forget to celebrate yourself today and every day!

Resources and Further Reading

Websites

Name of website: Cells Alive
Where is it? www.cellsalive.com
Who runs it? CELLS alive!
This is a really interesting site that is mostly about cells, but also has great ideas that will help you with almost any science fair project. They have lots of interesting pictures and you can even watch a bacterial colony grow real-time on their webcam, although you might not want to do it while you're eating!

Name of website: Kids' Health for Kids-The Game Closet
Where is it? http://kidshealth.org/kid/games/
Who runs it? The Nemours Foundation's Center for Children's Health Media
Want an easy and fun way to learn more about your health? Check out the games section where you'll find cool stuff like "Mission Nutrition" and "My Body Scavenger Hunt."

Name of website: Preteen Health Talk
Where is it? http://www.pamf.org/preteen/
Who runs it? The Palo Alto Medical Foundation
Find tons of information about your changing body. Also includes sections on your feelings, growing up, and sharing. Make sure to check out the interactive section on bullying.

Name of website: Professor Freedman's Math Help Pages

Where is it? www.mathpower.com

Who runs it? Professor Freedman, a faculty member at Camden County Community College in New Jersey. Professor Freedman does seem to really, really, really love math! This site is full of tips, links, and resources all about math, including lots of quizzes, and a section on making math fun.

Name of website: Young Women's Health

Where is it? www.youngwomenshealth.org

Who runs it? Center for Young Women's Health / Children's Hospital of Boston
A very extensive website with all sorts of information about young women's health. The information is broken up into larger categories like nutrition and fitness, emotional health, and development. There is some information here you might not find anywhere else: stuff like how to develop a healthy vegetarian diet suitable for a teen girl and a fun interactive lunch builder.

Name of website: Represent Magazine

Where is it? http://www.representmag.org/

Who runs it? The Center for Youth Communications
Although this publication is created by and for young women in foster care, even if that's not your particular situation, you might really enjoy this online magazine. There are sections written on development, friends, dating, addiction, and mental health, all by young people.

Name of website: Stop Bullying

Where is it? http://www.stopbullying.gov

Who runs it? The federal government's Bullying Prevention Steering Committee
This is the best place on the web to find reliable information about bullying: what it is, what it isn't, and what you can do about it. Look for the special resource sections that were put together with pre-teens in mind!

Name of website: Teen in Charge: Teen Health

Where is it? http://www.teensincharge.org/

Who runs it? The Chinese Community Health Resource Center

This site contains lots of great health information, including information about your body, your emotions, and videos about how to make healthy choices.

Name of website: Hardy Girls, Healthy Women

Where is it? http://www.hghw.org/content/tip-sheets

Who runs it? Hardy Girls Healthy Women, a nonprofit organization dedicated to the health and well being of girls and women.

Check out the great tip sheets for growing up to be a resilient and confident woman.

Name of website: Powered By Girl

Where is it? http://poweredbygirl.org/

Who runs it? The site is created by the Healthy Girls, Hardy Women organization, but most of the content on the site is created by pre-teen and teen girls.

This site contains fun and interesting writing and photos of ads that demean women and girls, and girls' hilarious take on them. It's a good way to start thinking about what the media tells you about you and your body and how you can think differently.

Name of website: Kidnetic

Where is it? http://www.kidnetic.com/

Who runs it? International Food Information Council Foundation

This is a colorful site about finding interesting and fun ways to eat healthy food and have fun moving your body. You can really spend some time here, poking around at all the pre-teen and teen-friendly information.

Books

Carlip, Hillary. **Girl Power: Young Women Speak Out!** New York: Warner, 1995. This is a collection of stories written by girls with all sorts of life situations. This book is really honest and touching, and might help you think in new ways about your life and your life situations.

Bolden, Tonya. **33 Things Every Girl Should Know: Stories, Songs, Poems, and Smart Talk by 33 Extraordinary Women.** New York: Crown, 1998
These selections, all by different authors, aim to offer advice that could help girls become more confident and give them a positive direction and outlook. The contributors, such as M.E. Kerr, Vera Wang, Wendy Wasserstein, and Faith Ringgold, represent a wide range of backgrounds and professions and include scientists, athletes, artists, sociologists, writers, and others.

About The Author And Illustrator

Kelli Dunham, RN, BSN is a nurse, a comedian, and author of three other books *How to Survive and Maybe Even Love Nursing School, How to Survive and Maybe Even Love Your Life as a Nurse,* as well as *The Boy's Body Book: Everything You Need to Know For Growing Up You,* also published by Applesauce Press. In her spare time she likes to read, skateboard, and embarrass her niece Viola when the whole family goes to the supermarket.

Laura Tallardy is an illustrator who graduated from Syracuse University's illustration program, and has vowed never to go anywhere that chilly again. She has illustrated the Lily Series, the Friend2Friend Club series, and is a frequent contributer to *Girl's Life* and *American Girl Magazine.* Currently she lives in Brooklyn with her favorite critter Bender.

INDEX

About Applesauce Press

Good ideas ripen with time. From seed to harvest, Applesauce Press creates books with beautiful designs, creative formats, and kid-friendly information. Like our parent company, Cider Mill Press Book Publishers, our press bears fruit twice a year, publishing a new crop of titles each spring and fall.

"Where Good Books Are Ready for Press"

Visit us on the web at
www.cidermillpress.com
or write to us at
12 Port Farm Road
Kennebunkport, Maine 04046